EssaySnark's Strategies for the
2014-'15 MBA Application for
YALE SCHOOL OF MANAGEMENT

EssaySnark's Strategies for the 2014-'15 MBA Application for YALE SCHOOL OF MANAGEMENT

by EssaySnark®

Snarkolicious Press

Paperback edition
first published June 29, 2014

Snarkolicious Press
P. O. Box 50021
Palo Alto, CA 94303

www.snarkoliciouspress.com

978-1-938098-25-3

© 2014 by EssaySnark®

Cover image © Eric Isselée, used under license from Fotolia.com

All rights reserved. EssaySnark is a registered trademark. No part of this book may be reproduced or transmitted in any form or by any means, electronic or mechanical, including photocopying, recording, transcribing, or by an information storage system, without permission from the publisher. Essay questions reproduced within are copyright Ross School of Business.

This publication is provided "as is", without warranty of any kind, either express or implied. The author and Snarkolicious Press assume no liability for errors or omissions in this publication or other documents which are referenced or linked to this publication. While we certainly hope that you will be successful in your quest for admission to an MBA program, we cannot offer any promises that you will be, whether or not you adopt the advice provided herein. In no event shall Snarkolicious Press or its authors, principals, subsidiaries, partners, or owners be liable for any special, incidental, indirect or consequential damages of any kind, or any damages whatsoever, arising out of or in conjunction with the use or performance of this information. Applicants to any graduate program or university should verify the school's policies, application requirements, processes, procedures, and other criteria. This publication could include technical or other inaccuracies or typographical errors. Changes are periodically added to the information herein; these changes will be incorporated into new editions of this publication. Thus, different versions or formats of this publication may include different information.

Look for other *SnarkStrategies Guides* (digital and paperback) at your favorite bookseller or on the EssaySnark blahg at http://essaysnark.com.

FOLLOW ESSAYSNARK ON TWITTER!

"Sweating the details
is more important than anything else."

Indra Nooyi
CEO of PepsiCo and SOM alum

We Believe that Yale Is on the Upswing

EssaySnark has been remiss. For many years now, we've failed to produce a SnarkStrategies Guide for the Yale School of Management. If you didn't know any better, you might think that we were dissing them on purpose. That's not the case – it's simply been a matter of limited resources available in Snarkville – but we're happy to finally have managed to get our act together and produce an essay guide for them. The timing is definitely right. You know that we don't care about rankings. But if we did... we'd be placing bets on Yale coming out higher and higher with each year going forward from now. Our belief is that they are going to be seen as more important in the MBA landscape as time moves on.

Why is that? If you've been doing any type of research about this school at all, then the answer to that should be obvious:

- They have a rockstar dean – Edward Snyder, who put Booth in the #1 position during his tenure as Chicago's dean (Snyder is the one who brought in the massive donation from Mr. Booth that resulted in the renaming of their school), and who has now been at SOM long enough to start making a difference there.

- They have a beautiful new glass building, which is high-tech and gorgeous and can accommodate expansion in the student body if they so choose – and which is a great pull to applicants who take the time to visit.

- Their average GPAs and GMAT scores have been ticking up – perhaps not what you want to hear as an applicant, but clear indication that they have the luxury of selectivity in their admissions processes.

At the same time: Yale suffered a slight dip in its application volume in the 2013-2014 application season at a time when most other schools saw an increase. This was probably due to their new-at-the-time requirement of an in-app video interview question that everyone completes. This is off trend from what most bschool are reporting. The videos at Yale may have been a turn-off to some. Yale typically gets about 2,800 applications, and they only lost around 2% of their volume last year, so it's not huge numbers we're talking about. However, Yale was one of the few schools to see a decrease in that app season and it's pretty easy to assume that it was due to the video question.

Whether or not a school is getting more applications each year actually shouldn't matter at all from your perspective. If you decide that this is the school for you, then fewer apps just means a little bit less competition, which is good news indeed. You don't want to go into this looking for the most popular school; you want to determine which is the right one for you, and Yale has some unique attributes that are exceptionally appealing to many people.

One of these factors is that Yale is attempting to be more transparent across the board – it's one of their themes and was a guiding principle in the design of that new building. They are attempting to extend that transparency to their admissions processes (though we find their website to be hard to navigate and not all that transparent in how they present their admissions info).

Snyder has also been emphasizing integration among the larger Yale campus community as an important trait of the school, and they are one of the few business schools that talks about humility in the same breath as leadership. While it's hard to point to any one business school that is wholly unique in its approach, there is enough different about the SOM of today that we can confidently apply that moniker to this school. In fact, as we will be discussing throughout this guide, Yale is one of the schools that comes closest, in our opinion, to the mission-driven education that we see happening at the Stanford GSB in California.

If you're applying to Yale now, you will be in a position to reap these benefits that will only be on the increase over time.

That wasn't always the case though, and for many years we cautioned Brave Supplicants to do their research carefully before committing to Yale. This school was a bit of a rudderless ship for many years, not having a permanent dean at the top, and struggling under the weight of their radical "integrated curriculum" when it was first introduced. Here in 2014, we feel that they are finding their sea legs and starting to come into their own, and we confidently predict that Yale will be moving up in reputation and regard compared to its peer schools in the coming years.

We're were not at all surprised when BusinessWeek placed Yale at #21 on their full-time MBA rankings in 2012. A lot has changed in a few years though, and we are dead certain that Yale will not be outside the Top 20 when the next rankings come out in Fall 2014.

This *SnarkStrategies Guide* will introduce you to some key differences at Yale compared to its peer schools, and offer advice and suggestions for how you can make the most of the opportunity to showcase your features to the admissions team in a way that convinces them that you belong there.

Because that's what's most important here: Showing how you are a fit to this special place.

What you won't get here

As with the other *SnarkStrategies Guides*, we're not going to tell you what you should write in your SOM essay. What we will do is explain some standard mistakes and help you know where to focus. But if you're looking for a "do this, don't do that, say this, don't say that" type of cheat-sheet approach to your essays, EssaySnark is bound to disappoint. We're not keen on the idea of spoonfeeding anyone the answers; not that there are any "answers" anyway. Applying to bschool is just as much about figuring out who you are, as it is in figuring out what a school is about. You need to do the work to uncover the truth on both dimensions in order to have a shot at success with this differentiated program.

You can find helpful material about Yale on the EssaySnark blahg at essaysnark.com – and even more so by traveling to New Haven to visit the school. This is *highly* recommended if you can pull it off. The best way to understand what a school is about is to visit them and talk to students and professors and other members of their community. We'll share what we know about the SOM but you'll be in a much stronger position if you do this firsthand research yourself.

Of course, if EssaySnark can help, please don't hesitate to reach out – try us on Twitter https://twitter.com/essaysnark or email us at gethelpnow@essaysnark.com if we can be of service.

Table of Contents

Who Is a Good Fit for Yale?..1
For Whom is Yale a Good Fit?..3
    Recruiting and Yale Career Services..6
    Which schools are similar?...8
    The Yale Integrated Curriculum...10
What's Important at Yale...14
    Yale and extracurriculars...16
Gaining the Best Advantage in Your Yale Application..18
    The core of a successful SOM strategy...19
    Do you "have" to visit Yale before applying?...21
Yale Evaluation Criteria..23
    GMAT..23
    Grades..25
    Older Applicant...26
    Reapplicants..27
The SOM Application..28
    Career Goals and Yale..29
Your Yale Essay...32
    Two common mistakes, and tactics for dealing with them................................32
    What is the best topic to use for this essay?..35
    How to structure it?..38
    How should you write the Yale Essay?..39
    Can you reuse your Harvard essay for Yale?..41
    Can you reuse your Yale essay for Harvard?..41
    Can you reuse your Yale essay for anything else?..41
The Optional Essay...43
Recommendations...44
The Video Essay Questions..46
    Sample questions from past seasons..47
    General tips for the Yale SOM video essays...48
Interviews..50
What to Do Next...51

Who Is a Good Fit for Yale?

We'll let the SOM answer that themselves: Here is a question that they've asked in their online applications in recent years.

> Below is a list of some of the qualities that describe Yale SOM students and alumni. Please review the list and check off the four (4) qualities on the list that you feel best describe you. Please note that there are no right or wrong answers here. We are not looking for any specific qualities, simply trying to get a better sense of you.

- Adaptable
- Analytical
- Conscientious
- Creative
- Hard-working
- Humble
- Inquisitive
- Intuitive
- Level-headed
- Open-minded
- Persistent
- Positive
- Quick-thinking
- Resilient
- Self-motivated
- Smart
- Socially adept
- Versatile

Which one of those resonate with you? Do a quick self-assessment and identify the qualities that you feel describe you. These are traits you'll want to be highlighting in your Yale application wherever possible.

If you can present a story in your Yale essay that demonstrates how you have some of these qualities, you're going to be helping yourself immensely.

We'll use this list for our first app development suggestion to you.

Snarky Strategy #1

As you're completing your brainstorming exercises and thinking of possible topics for your Yale essay and interview, review that list of qualities and traits to see how you can demonstrate who you are to the adcom.

You shouldn't be trying to write to the list – that would be the complete backwards way to go about it. But what you can do is, as you identify possible topics for your Yale essay, you can test them against that list, to see what qualities each of them could possibly be communicating about you. That's a great way to go in making sure that you're selecting stories that will put you in the strongest light for this school.

For Whom is Yale a Good Fit?

In other words, what career paths are most appropriate for a Yale MBA? The answer, as you probably expected, is "many."

Yale has a reputation as the "non-profit school" and while they are much more than that, they definitely do still get lots of applicants interested in social ventures and public service. Their tagline, after all, is that they develop leaders "for business and society"; they have it built into their mission. If that's where you're coming from, and that's where your heart is, you're going to be in good company at the SOM. The only downside to trying for Yale if you're a nonprofit person is that there's lots and lots of others "like you" applying, so it can be harder to stand out from the crowd. The best part? That Yale is well equipped to helping the non-traditional bschool student, and you may find that you have better support to deal with the challenging business curriculum than you might at another school.

Yale is also geographically advantaged, being right in between New York City and Boston, and so they have plenty of students drawn to Wall Street and financial services, and to the startup and biotech hubs in Cambridge. There are also some distinct niches at Yale, such as the opportunity to leverage the performing arts specialization at Yale's renowned School of Drama. Dean Snyder talks up a storm about how you can take advantage of all the resources within the entire Yale University community, so if you are interested in leveraging the strengths of Yale and performing arts – or Yale and law, or any other area – then it's a great time to be applying.

As many schools do, Yale puts an emphasis on leadership in a global context. Dean Snyder is making it a hallmark of his tenure that Yale SOM increases its connections to other business schools of the world. Given that this is a young business school with a comparatively small alumni network, this push to increase the SOM's presence in other countries through partnerships makes sense as a strategic move.

Of course, if you've been doing the MBA circuit at all, then you've already become familiar with the buzzwords of "leadership" and "global opportunity" that spew forth from the marketing materials of pretty much every top school. It's a given that U.S. bschools put an emphasis on leadership and that they're touting their international programs. Just because Dean Snyder is talking up these goals for the SOM doesn't mean that you have to have these goals for yourself. It's not necessary for you to check all of those boxes in how you present yourself in your app; don't try to shoehorn yourself into some mold that you believe the school wants. It's not like you have to want to lead a multinational conglomerate in its expansion in emerging markets in order to qualify for a place at Yale (in fact, such a career goal in an essay would in most cases be seen as woefully overconfident). If you genuinely have an interest in that sort of thing, great! Yale could be a perfect fit for you, and properly-articulated goals about those interests will serve you well.

If you're interested in entrepreneurship, we are not going to discourage you from trying at Yale, but we do need to caution you that it doesn't seem as if the SOM has the deepest set of resources and support available for entrepreneurs as other schools can offer. You may be more on your own if you try to build a startup out of bschool. There is certainly a long history of startups out of Yale, including HonestTea in the '90s and the MBA admissions and test prep company Veritas Prep. However, we've been more impressed in recent years by the breadth and depth of resources and the overall ecosystem of entrepreneurship that other schools have exhibited (NYU comes to mind).

That being said: Clearly Yale is not afraid of innovation, and change is in the air in New Haven these days. This is in evidence by the new building, and also by the changes they made to their application. The interview questions that Yale pioneered in the 2012 admissions cycle and then standardized in 2013 were considered fairly revolutionary; Kellogg introduced them in the same year, however we understand that the Kellogg version suffered from numerous technical issues that really stressed out the applicants. We didn't hear that complaint nearly as much about the Yale video questions.

Yale also decided to ditch its requirement for the TOEFL exam for non-native English speakers in 2013, which is great. The schools can always get a feel for a candidate's communication skills from the GMAT essay section (they don't always trust that the application essays were actually written by the candidates themselves). They also use the interview for this, to evaluate English skills. And, now, Yale has the video questions which give them a direct look at their applicants. This type of innovative – while you may not see it as all that radical, in the sphere of MBA admissions it's kind of unique – this gives a hint that the school is embracing innovation as part of its mission, which is certainly a good sign. You definitely want to go to a bschool that is walking its talk, and we feel that Yale SOM is doing that.

Along those lines, what you will also find at Yale is a focus on collaboration throughout the entire educational experience. This comes through in their integrated curriculum, which requires the faculty to work together in new ways – ways that don't necessarily come naturally to tenured professors.

In order to offer a truly integrated approach to teaching their subjects, each of the professors has had to get together with their peers to design new coursework and lesson plans. This means that you're less likely to encounter a "stuck" professor at Yale (meaning, someone who's made it to the pinnacle of his field and is now coasting there). While you're still likely to see the typical curmudgeonly prof, due to this curricular innovation, Yale professors must be more flexible than you might find at many other schools. One professor claims that "every class is in beta" at Yale, meaning it's still a work-in-progress. If you're not comfortable with change then this means you may not be the best fit for Yale. Correspondingly, the Yale admissions team values flexibility in their applicants, because they know that the bschool experience requires significant adaptation, especially as this school is in the process of reinventing itself.

In fact, one of the key challenges that you'll have in working through your Yale application will be in doing some intense self-reflection and introspection, in order to understand your own value system and finding ways to present that where possible in your essay. Yale wants to see emotional intelligence, adaptability, and maturity in its applicants, and they definitely need to get a sense for why you're choosing them for your graduate education. Even though the main essay question asks about a story of contribution to an organization, you can absolutely still use that essay to talk about what you are seeking in the future with your MBA. It will undoubtedly come up in the interview as well. These things can't be faked with canned answers. You'll need to dig deep to uncover the reasons for yourself.

In terms of appropriate career paths that can be best supported by a Yale MBA, the options are still pretty standard to what you'll see at any top school, with perhaps a slightly different mix and a weighting towards the do-gooder roles like education and non-profit. (BTW, the fact that slightly more people go into fields not known for paying the big bucks means that average exit salaries are somewhat lower at the SOM. Take that into consideration as you review the statistics.)

When considering Yale's support for international candidates, it's worth noting that Yale University offers a no-cosigner needed loan for SOM students, which is generally approved upon application, no questions asked. This is a very different situation than you'll be faced with at some other schools, where international students are practically on their own in coming up with funding.

Since we're talking about financial aid: Yale does not offer any need-based aid, however they have lots of merit-based fellowships, and they are also quite generous in their consideration and allocation of money to grads working in non-profit and service-based industries through their loan forgiveness program. Many schools offer something similar however Yale seems a bit more liberal in how that money is allocated than we've seen at other places. This is helpful for those considering a post-MBA career path that may not be as lucrative.

So to summarize the types of applicant for whom Yale might be a good choice:

- those coming from non-profit and service-based professions, including education, Peace Corps, etc.
- military candidates
- anyone who wants to go into consulting
- to a lesser degree: anyone who wants to go to Wall Street
- international applicants, especially anyone not from the standard Indian pool
- Americans who want to pursue an international career (this candidate profile should get an especially warm welcome)
- anyone with maturity and flexibility and resilience, who is ready to take an active role in his or her graduate business education

Who might not be a good fit for Yale

A quick comment on one type of person who may find Yale to be frustrating: Someone who studied business, economics or finance during college.

The reason for this? Yale doesn't allow you to test out of the core courses, and theirs seems to be the *least flexible* curriculum of their peer schools.

Whereas a school like Booth will give you different options on how you can satisfy your corporate finance requirement, based on whether you've had exposure to the topic before or if it's brand new to you, Yale doesn't let you. You'll be going through all of the core with your classmates, no matter what your level of expertise is to the subject. This may create some real boredom and frustration, and some students feel that they're wasting their time. We're sure that Yale has a reason for this policy (probably to help cohesion of the experience within the integrated curriculum) yet it's one case where it may not seem to be student-focused.

Recruiting and Yale Career Services

Yale gets somewhat fewer of the traditional recruiters that you may see at other schools; for example, we've heard that Apple does not formally recruit there (which is weird, since former dean Joel Podolny went to Apple after his departure from the school).

That doesn't mean you can't get a job at Apple out of Yale SOM. The Career Services team will work with you to submit for openings at such companies, even if they're not participating in the SOM's on-campus recruiting program. It's still very possible to get an offer through those channels and grads do it every year, but some people may feel more comfortable or confident if their career goals involve a certain company in applying to schools where that company already has committed to source applicants as part of its own annual recruiting process.

You certainly get a lot of consultants coming out of the SOM, and based on the reasonable proximity to New York City, plenty of financial services types too. However, we have heard anecdotally that there just aren't that many resources available to those interested in finance at Yale. They are still lacking the deep connections to the major firms and one student even said that there is no on-campus recruiting from any big buy-side player at the SOM. You should consider this to be mere rumor since we didn't get it from the school itself, but it's definitely something that you need to research carefully if you're thinking about going to Yale for finance — ESPECIALLY if you are a career changer. If you've already worked in the field, it may be less of an issue for you.

Some say that Cornell has better support for finance people than Yale does in the career services space. Yale is physically closer to New York City but if they don't have the big guns deployed at that sector from a recruiting perspective then it's going to be harder for someone to land the cherry job from this school.

That doesn't mean that there's a dearth of opportunities coming out of Yale — just that you need to investigate your options. Along those lines, another warning that we'd offer is if you're interested in building a business through bschool. Just like at every school these days, entrepreneurship is increasingly popular at Yale — but as we already mentioned, this isn't the first school that we think of when entrepreneurship comes up as a real near-term career goal for a BSer. If you're serious about starting a venture, we believe that other places may be more advantageous to you.

One positive takeaway from the Yale recruiting statistics is that there are lots and lots of Yale grads going into lots and lots of different jobs. The type and number are highly varied. About 80% of the employers hired just one Yalie. This means that there are a huge number of very diverse opportunities that can be explored and achieved from a Yale MBA. Yale Career Services manages things differently, both in reaction to some challenges that the school has faced in recent years, and also as part of the SOM's focus on innovation. Being a younger, and smaller, MBA program means that this school is more nimble, and this is in evidence in its Career Services structure and approach.

When there is such diversity in the employer pool (and it changes every year) then that means that these companies are not likely going to be tapped for surveys from the likes of BusinessWeek and other publications that are designing rankings of schools. BusinessWeek in particular has weighted its ranking significantly towards recruiters' opinions, which has probably been to the SOM's detriment. There has been less data available to sum up about Yale in those (already artificial) comparison lists. This is why one school – like Yale – can show up in such a different position on the different rankings produced by different companies.

Back to Yale and career services:

If you go through an info session with this school, they're likely to talk up their career services approach quite significantly. In fact, they may even spend a good chunk of time on it, discussing their emphasis on building transferable skills in their students, and a focus on the employers' needs and deploying curriculum to support those needs throughout the MBA experience.

This focus on career services is to your benefit, since it:

a) Gives you a chance during an info session to ask some direct questions about their methods and resources, in case what we've said in this guide has raised any doubts for you (though you should typically save personal or very specific questions about a certain sector until after the presentation is over, when you can approach the presenter individually); and

b) Tells you that Yale cares a lot about career services and how it places its graduates.

All schools do care about that of course, since they are in the business of matchmaking grads to companies, however not all schools talk it up quite as much, in quite the same language, in their info sessions, so we just wanted to mention this so that you can be on the lookout.

We do believe that Yale's methods in career services are differentiated compared to some schools, and it's a great place for you if you don't want to follow the herd. However, if you actually *do* want to use bschool the way a huge number of people use bschool – to break into finance especially – then just take a close look at how this school, and others, might serve you best in that regard.

Which schools are similar?

When we look at peer schools to the SOM, we're most struck by the similarities with Tuck – at least, in terms of location, and the numbers.

Both Tuck and Yale get about the same number of applications each year (hovering in the 2,500 to 2,800 range in recent years). Both have about the same-sized class (typically 275 to 300, though Yale is well positioned to increase theirs right now). Both care about the school community and focus on culture and fit as a key ingredient of their evaluation matrix. Both are housed in venerable Ivy League research institutions with great history.

The similarities break down at a certain point – Tuck is one of the oldest business schools in the world and they're big on tradition, with very stable leadership in Dean Paul Danos who announced that he'll be stepping down in 2015 after twenty years in the role). Yale, by contrast, is on the opposite end of that "age" and "stability" spectrum. But these schools are more comparable than not, and we find that many applicants who are interested in one are also interested in the other – and often, people who are successful at one are also able to get an offer from the other as well.

Which they end up choosing, when faced with that abundance of riches, is a very personal decision, so we're not about to tell you which is "better." That will come down to your own experiences with the respective schools and what resonates with you as a future student.

We see a lot of overlap between those interested in NYU and those interested in Yale, though the actual bschool experience at these two schools is quite different – not just due to the obvious city-versus-not experience (New Haven is a fairly small town) but also because Stern offers a more traditional curriculum with a structured core, compared to Yale's integrated curriculum with the raw cases. (If you don't know what those two terms are, you need to do more research to understand how Yale does things; it's different.) The admissions statistics are also quite different between these two schools, with NYU being a third larger in size and getting a commensurately larger number of apps.

Also like Yale, Cornell is another Ivy League university with a business school that's not quite as well regarded as its university peers are; Cornell and Yale both are places where the parent institution has a much better reputation among the general public than the business school has among the MBA community. That doesn't mean that Cornell and Yale aren't good MBA programs, it just means that some of their prestige is the halo effect of the parent institution. It's actually quite a bit easier to get an admit from Cornell than it is from Yale; the admissions experience is not nearly as competitive at Johnson. Culturally the schools are somewhat similar though also quite different, so this is again another time when visiting each can be very helpful if you're considering where you might fit best.

Another two schools that are reasonably similar to Yale in terms of culture and values are Berkeley-Haas, as well as Stanford GSB. Obviously the West Coast of the U.S. is a totally different lifestyle and culture (as well as climate!!) than the Northeast and this does play in to the bschool experience which differs markedly at each of these three schools, yet there is some overlap as well. We believe that Yale's Dean Snyder is gunning for an image of "the Stanford of the East Coast" with how he's positioning things at the SOM, but that's just complete conjecture on our part (we certainly never heard him or his staff say anything point-blank in that regard). In terms of the values and the focus on mission and culture, we do see similarities and all three of these schools are worth exploring if these themes resonate with you. It's typically easier to gain acceptance to Yale than it is to either of these two California schools however – and it's not very easy to do that – so don't be lulled into some false sense of simplicity in thinking that Berkeley might be a "safety school" to Yale and Stanford; it just doesn't work that way (we discuss the reasons why in the Berkeley-Haas essay guide, in case you're interested).

We're offering these points of similarity between these various schools in an effort to help you understand which others you may be a good fit for – assuming, of course, that what we've said thus far about Yale gets you excited to believe that you're a fit for SOM.

The Yale Integrated Curriculum

We already mentioned this multiple times yet it's one of the most important aspects of the Yale experience so it's worth calling out separately. Yale is doing an experiment with its unique approach to business education. This is still relatively new, in the broader scheme of things, and nobody has actual data on how it's turning out. The Class of 2008 was the first cohort to go through the Integrated Curriculum, so they have not even been in the workforce for a decade, and they were turned out into their new careers at a very inopportune time – and even though the concept and overall structure of Yale's program has remained the same, the curriculum has changed radically from how it was first implemented till today. In fact, one professor said that the curriculum at Yale is "always in beta" and up to 40% of his class changes each time he teaches it. One Yale student said that the school is a "start-up" – meaning that it's a little chaotic, and there are amazing opportunities and a breathless experience (http://som.yale.edu/yale-som-start-business-school). But it's also easy to get overwhelmed.

Here's the basic schematic of the first year of Yale's Integrated Curriculum, so you get a bird's eye view of how it works:

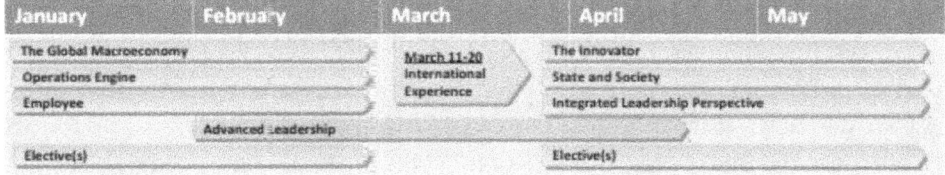

And here's how they depicted it in 2012, just so you can see how it's evolving:

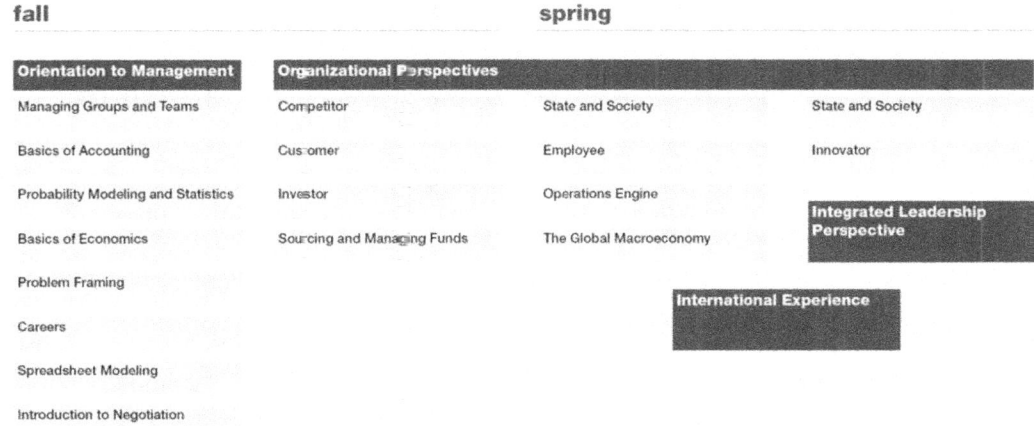

The biggest difference is how they've pulled the leadership content front-and-center and made it part of the entirety of the first-year experience, rather than being tacked on at the end as it was initially.

Here's a write-up from a Yale student in December 2013 on his (her?) experience with the integrated curriculum:

http://som.yale.edu/whats-yale-som-really?blog=3490

The *subjects* that you will learn at Yale are the same as at other places, but it's the *perspectives* that they're doing differently. But keep in mind, that nothing at any business school is wholly unique. Berkeley-Haas has a first-term class called Problem Framing, Problem Solving. Stanford has been taking a different approach to leadership training for ages. The way that Yale is packaging up and delivering their content is the main point of distinction. We're not saying it's better nor worse than any other schools, but it is certainly being marketed differently, and the overriding philosophy is differentiated. In terms of going to class and working in groups and studying for exams? You'll be doing that pretty much exactly the same at the SOM as you would be anywhere else.

That being said, the integrated curriculum is so fundamental to the Yale experience that it makes sense to mention it in an essay – if you can. At the same time, it's something that EVERYBODY mentions, since they hear the adcom talk about it. What will set you apart is if you can reference the Integrated curriculum *in a way that shows that you really know what it's about, what the advantages are, and how it might benefit YOU in the pursuit of your goals and objectives.* Very few people do this. We see "integrated curriculum" and "raw cases" bandied about in essays but a superficial reference to those things is just a starting point.

This is an area where you'll benefit most from talking to students and alumni, to understand how this works and what it means. The downside of course is that any SOM alumni only has that one point of reference; they never experienced the standard approach to curricular design that most other schools deploy, so it's not like they can offer a holistic view of its advantages.

And, you need to be careful about wholesale lifting what someone else says into your own essays as a reason for yourself to want to go to Yale. You would want to, ahem, *integrate* what you learn from others into your own thought process and value system, and demonstrate THAT to the adcom in how you talk about these features of their program.

Along with the integrated curriculum and Dean Snyder's focus on "integration" within the larger Yale University campus as well as within an international network of other graduate business schools, a separate but not distinct aspect of Yale that they're proud of is their Leadership Development Program. This is one of the more extensive versions of formal leadership training that you'll see at the top schools; they're not the only one who's doing it this way, but they are taking it seriously and devoting a lot of resources to it – and a lot of time within the two-year MBA experience. This stems from the fact that leadership is learned not through books and lectures but by doing. It's also got a great focus on bringing in outside views so that you can learn more about yourself. It's sort of how Stanford approaches the topic, with 360-degree assessments and many touchpoints of observation and feedback. Expect to be made uncomfortable at many times throughout the Yale experience when you learn stuff about yourself that you were clueless on. You need to have some resilience and an interest in personal development in order to be a good fit to this system.

What's Important at Yale

Having that resilience will be useful to you as a Yale SOM student. Among other traits that Yale looks for in its candidates are *authenticity* and *humility* and *evidence of leadership* – and more and more, they're emphasizing intellectual capability too.

That must come through in your app.

What is starting to matter more at Yale are higher GPAs and better GMAT scores. We saw a marked emphasis on GPA starting with the 2012 application season, and this is borne out by an average GPA that's greater than 3.5, which is on par with schools like NYU and above Tuck and Columbia.

Which is the perfect segue into a discussion of the whole point of this guide: What does it take to get in, and how do you position yourself to showcase your best qualities?

- Leadership and Impact – What contributions have you made in the different environments of which you've been a part?

- Intellectual Ability – Have you done the work in school and on your GMAT? Are you prepared for the rigors of a top MBA program?

- Emotional Intelligence (EQ) – Are you mature, capable, a team player?

- Diversity – Do you bring something new to the community? These can come into play through a variety of dimensions, though particularly valued would be either an international awareness – Are you well-traveled and culturally aware? And/or social impact – Are you striving to do good in the world?

For reasons unknown to us, Yale SOM has struggled to attract underrepresented minorities. They have an abysmal rate of less than 10% of the student population made up of African-Americans and Hispanics and it's hovered as low as 7% in some years. We took them to task for this in a write-up in 2013 here:

https://medium.com/this-could-be-better/top-american-business-school-10-minority-enrollment-thats-diversity-ec3d490ad3d0

We're honestly not sure why this low minority enrollment has been the reality at Yale, except that it's difficult at many top schools, and that it could simply be a self-perpetuating cycle: Few minorities on campus means that when a prospective applicant encounters the school and doesn't see many others "like him" around, that he's (or she's) discouraged from applying.

We know that Yale is well aware of this issue and they are a member of the Consortium and they were even a founder of MLT (Management Leaders for Tomorrow), plus they host the standard Diversity Days on campus in the Fall — so there's evidence that they've been working to address this imbalance. But you should know about it in advance, in case this measure of diversity matters to you.

If you happen to be an African-American or Hispanic, then you are guaranteed to receive a warm welcome from the SOM admissions team. You can't skate in with substandard stats or massive holes in your profile just because you're a minority applicant, but you will definitely be actively courted if you express interest in attending the Yale School of Management.

What else are they on the lookout for? Well, if you attend an info session with the Yale School of Management, you are quite likely to hear them talk about emotional intelligence. Yale and NYU are pushing this term more than many schools do. They really want to admit only adults into their programs (and we don't mean "adults" only by chronological age).

Another critical angle for you to impart as you express yourself in your application: Do you know what this school is about? What outreach have you done? What can you say about your reasons for wanting to go there? The Yale adcom will need to be convinced that you understand what they're about and that you are choosing them for their values and strengths.

By highlighting the activities you've been involved with in your life and the interests you have, you'll be able to communicate that you share those values. Your essays, your resume, and your recommendations are all places where this can come through. You needn't make this part of your platform if it's not naturally so — please don't artificially try to inject these qualities if they're not already in evidence within your background and history. If you do have some of this naturally in your profile then it is nice to highlight it within your application assets, particularly if it's related to your future goals.

Related but distinct from this is a shared trait within the SOM culture: one of *community* Regardless of your background, this is one of the most important aspects of your profile that you'll want to highlight and leverage throughout your application.

Snarky Strategy #2

The SOM culture is one of authenticity and transparency. Above all, be yourself in your essay/application and especially in your interview.

Yale and extracurriculars

Given Yale's reputation as a non-profit school, people often feel like they need to demonstrate all their altruism and do-gooder-ness on the application. Sometimes people stretch to show that they've been involved in all these impressive activities over their lives.

This is not the best strategy.

First of all, if you have a huge number of activities and volunteer stuff that you're touting on the app, they simply won't believe you.

Anyone applying to Yale with any chance of success is going to be coming from a job that occupies a big chunk of their time. If you have all this freedom to also be volunteering with five different social service agencies, and you are actually making a significant contribution to each one, then you're really not pushing it in your career. There's also a bunch of candidates with jobs that aren't conducive to volunteering. Military service is one that comes to mind (though we're not letting you military guys off the hook with this; if you can find a way to do some formal volunteer effort of some kind, it would make your candidacy more distinctive and help you stand out from the crowd).

Other candidate types who tend to be interested in Yale are already coming from the volunteer world. If you work in non-profit, or education, then you're already "giving back." (This is also true of the military guys, obviously, which is why the schools don't actually need to see that much more in the way of volunteer experience from that cohort – though it can still help you stand out, since it's unusual.)

OK, enough parentheticals. Here's the deal with Yale and volunteer experience:

1. Given their mission around teaching leaders for business "and society", then it would certainly help your candidacy if you have some volunteer experience to report. This is more true of American candidates, since we have a culture of volunteerism. If you're coming from another part of the world, maybe this element isn't quite so important in your profile – though it always adds.

2. Your volunteer experiences should communicate more of who you are. The organizations you choose to associate with and dedicate your time to will reveal your priorities in life, and your values. And Yale likes values.

3. The work you do should hopefully have some impact; it should also be a long-term engagement where you spend a decent chunk of time on a regular basis. Intermittently or one-off volunteering doesn't move the needle and in some cases should just be omitted from the application.

4. If you have too many activities to report, you might raise minor red flags. The adcom just won't believe you. This is too often a place where people stuff stuff; these experiences typically cannot be verified, and so the adcom is naturally skeptical. Be selective in what you report and how you report it. Choose wisely.

5. You don't have to have just formal 501(c)(3) activities going on; it's not necessary that you devote all your time to some official non-profit with tax-exempt status from the IRS. You can still communicate your values and what's important to you by mentioning the sports you play, your hobbies, or however else you spend your time. What's important is that you care about it, and it reflects your interests. These items should be at the bottom of the resume since they offer a fuller picture of who you are and how you spend your time.

Gaining the Best Advantage in Your Yale Application

First let's get the round question out of the way:

Snarky Strategy #3

Apply in Round 1 if you can.
(Reapplicants especially should apply in Round 1.)

Round 1 is an advantage, and it can help a lot to apply early in the season, regardless of your profile. As other schools do, Yale gets more applications in Round 2 so it's more competitive. If you're coming from the non-profit sector that's slightly more crowded at Yale, then a Round 1 app will be even more important, as you can better stand out from the crowd if you apply earlier in the season.

The main benefit of doing Yale in Round 1?

It's an earlier deadline than many other schools.

So why is that a benefit?

Well, Yale has a pretty awesome essay question this year. Do a good job on that, and you might be able to reuse the story you present to Yale in some other schools' essays, too. You also need to map out your career goals for Yale (even though there's no formal essay about them, we do expect that they will ask you to specify your goals within the online application – as of this writing, that app hasn't been released, but they had that before). So you'll be able to use a lot of the hard thinking that you'll need to put into that Yale Round 1 app for the other Round 1 schools you'll be tackling.

Doing your Yale application will help you answer these questions:

Why do you want an MBA?

Or another way to look at it: What do you lack that the MBA will give you?

The answer that solves both riddles: What are your career goals?

Your career goals should be easily understandable, based on where you sit today – they don't have to be only an extension of what you've done thus far but they need to make sense, given your existing career trajectory.

And finally, the question that shows how you'd be an asset to the school if they accept you: What have you done in your career to date that's totally freakin' awesome?

Nail those questions well and you're setting yourself up for success with writing pretty much every other school's application, too.

And oh yeah: If you're a reapplicant, then it's going to be much more credible for you to jam a Round 1 app if you're trying to communicate how much you're committed to Yale. Round 2 is acceptable as a reapplicant but it's really not what we recommend. We touch more on reapplicants at Yale on page 27 and we also have a separate Reapplicant's Guide to help you out if you're in this situation.

The core of a successful SOM strategy

With your Yale application, you need to do what you need to do with many bschool apps: You need to explain why you want an MBA, in the context of what you want to do with the degree when you graduate – and you need to show how you're qualified to go pursue those goals, based on some relevant background experience or achievement that you'll be able to tout in the essay.

Even if you don't end up writing lots and lots about your actual goals, you need to put enough thought into them that the adcom will be able to easily accept them when they read them. You need to have enough details to show how these goals are real for you, that you've done some research and didn't just come up with this whole idea about getting an MBA when you fell out of bed yesterday morning.

Then, the main goal of the Yale essay is to demonstrate how you're in a position to make such a jump or transition to your intended future goals, based on your background and the experiences you bring to the table. This essay is an opportunity to demonstrate that you will hit the ground running and actively engage. If you pick a story that shows you being proactive, being a problem-solver, being someone on whom others can rely, then it elevates your standing in the eyes of the adcom. They want people who will roll up their hands and contribute. If your story also shows you as being creative, as having a level head in times of extreme stress, as bringing people together, and/or as someone who brings new value to situations, then even better.

Yes, it's possible to do all these things in a 500-word essay.

You should strive to have examples in your app – in the essay, or somewhere depicted on the resume, and also hopefully in the recommendations – that show you're a go-getter, that you're proactive, that you participate in the world around you. There are an infinite number of ways to demonstrate this trait, but it's important to recognize that Yale is a dynamic and often complex environment, and the adcom wants to make sure they admit people who will exceed there. We've heard that up to 40% of your grades at Yale are based on classroom participation. They don't want to let you in if you're not going to be comfortable speaking up and being part of the conversation.

You also need to come across as a real person. Sometimes we see essays written for bschool apps that appear to have come from a robot. People sound like automatons in their writing, or they trot out the million-dollar words that nobody ever uses in everyday speech, in an attempt to sound smart. Keep your thesaurus lodged comfortably in its dusty spot on your bookshelf. Don't be tempted to use lofty writing and fancy phrases. Write in a simple way that authentically sounds like you – with clear examples and good stories – and you'll be setting yourself up for success.

One test, that all admissions officers agree with? Have someone close to you – a family member or dear friend – read your essay, and tell you if it sounds like you.

If not, then you've assumed an affected voice, and it's not doing you any favors.

This is the only time when EssaySnark feels that it's valuable to have a family member read an essay, by the way. Typically getting your mom to look at your MBA apps is a recipe for trouble. We would never suggest that your close friend or family member could offer real value to the CONTENT of your essays. Please don't solicit them for help on what you should be saying. Unless your brother-in-law is Bruce DelMonico, then steer clear of asking for his input on what you're writing (of course, we'd assume that Bruce DelMonico would refuse to give feedback on your essays, regardless of your relationship to him).

Another point of this whole "authenticity" thing that Yale cares about is, do you really want to go to this school? The adcoms have this weird sixth sense where they can pick up on it if you're faking.

Yale knows that they haven't hit the upper echelons of the bschool rankings in a long time, and they're sensitive to the fact that many people think of them as a "safety school."

Believe us, Yale is not a safety school – not when you consider their admissions patterns. It is *difficult* to get an offer at this school. They screen carefully for any number of things, including an evaluation of sincerity of interest. One easy way for them to know if you are really sold on Yale or if you're just adding them to the list of possibilities is the degree to which you have done your homework. Have you reached out to students and alumni? Have you attended info sessions? Have you visited campus?

No, it's totally not mandatory to visit New Haven – but if you do, you are going to be blown away by the Yale SOM facilities.

The new building is just gorgeous.

The town of New Haven is your typical New England hamlet; there is an almost-city feel to parts of it but much of the area surrounding Yale University is a mixture of incredibly quant brownstones and old brick buildings... plus, unfortunately, quite a bit of blight. There is tremendous poverty in New Haven. More than one SOM student has expressed dismay at the situation. It's not the nicest environment overall, frankly. You need to be aware of this, too.

We're not suggesting that you would write about that part of the New Haven reality in your essays, but it would certainly be valuable to your research purposes to both see the incredible building that you'd be going to school in for two years – and to understand the overall community that it's a part of. Both aspects matter. A lot.

Do you "have" to visit Yale before applying?

Totally do not. But it would help if you did. And you'll likely enjoy it a lot.

The Yale faculty and staff always impress us. (We can't say that about every school, frankly.) There is an energy and an enthusiasm at this school that can become very infectious. The building. The newness. The excitement.

It's not so easy to get to Yale. If you're flying in, you either need to go to Boston or to New York and then you can take the train. It ends up being quite a haul just to get on campus. There's also an airport in some nearby Connecticut town but it only has like two flights a day. You need to commit significant time just in terms of travel to make it there.

Keep that in mind in your decision-making about which school, by the way. You'll likely be on the train quite a bit to get to different industry events and recruiting activities in those other cities if you end up at Yale. And if you are bringing a (non-student) partner to bschool with you, then it can be a bit of a drag for them if they need to do a lot of work-related travel.

The main reason that we'd encourage you to visit is for your own purposes.

You can certainly learn a lot about Yale from reading about it – this book, for example, and other resources. But you won't get a true sense for the community and the opportunity without a visit.

And it will also educate you on the downsides that we've mentioned. Since those exist, too.

After that main benefit of visiting, in terms of how much better educated you'll be on whether this is the right school for you, the other huge gain you'll see is all the information you can integrate into your application and interview. Having a first-hand experience with the school can go so far. It can really make an application convincing.

If you cannot make it to campus, don't worry; it's not held against you in any way at all. We promise that's the case.

Those who are able to visit are not put at the front of the line, just because they got on a plane and a train and a taxi cab to get there.

The opportunity to visit will provide you with more insights – and, most likely, more enthusiasm – for what this school is about. That's where the real advantage comes in.

If you can get there, then do it. Summertime is nice, though there aren't many students around, and no classes to sit in on. Don't push out your apps to Round 2 just so that you can manage the on-campus experience before you apply. If the timing works out for you though, then definitely make a point of getting up there. You'll likely be really impressed.

When should you visit?

The tricky part is timing. Many of you are reading this Guide in preparation for a Round 1 application. The ideal time to visit in order for the experience to benefit your apps is before you finish the essays – you want to have your core platform established and maybe the first set of drafts done, and then visit the school, go through the campus tour and class visit, and talk to people. Then you'll be armed and ready with everything you need in order to tailor the essays just so.

The problem is that you'll be writing essays for your Round 1 app in the summertime – and class visits aren't available till the Fall. Bschool students are off doing their summer internships in the summer, so the campus is mostly a ghost town. Attending a class and talking to students is the most valuable part of the school visit experience, and you wouldn't get any of that if you go in the summer. We are most definitely not suggesting that you should delay your application until after you'd had a chance to go to the school. So basically that means, for many people, you'll skip the visit – or hopefully you'll plan for it later.

A Snarky Caveat

Visiting Yale is optional (though recommended). Researching the school and knowing why you're interested in them is not.

Yale Evaluation Criteria

Here's what we're seeing over the course of the past few years:

Yale has become more of a stickler for a high GPA.

They also care about GMAT. but due to the realities of their applicant pool and the larger number of non-trads applying to Yale, the adcom continues to be lenient on the absolute numbers, and the breakdown, of the GMAT score.

They also will accept a GRE, though in previous years they have expressed a slight preference for the GMAT if you're someone who has very little obvious quant abilities in evidence elsewhere in the profile. So, if you studied French art history in college, and have been working in a non-profit for the past four years, then it would help your candidacy to take the GMAT instead of the GRE.

The main exception to that guideline is if you're also applying to a joint degree program, in which case the GRE could be smarter only because some other grad programs only take the GRE and not the GMAT.

The adcom will understand, if that's the case. But for most people the GMAT is the better choice.

GMAT

The average GMAT score for Yale's class of 2015 is 714 – though it was as high as 720 in recent years. It's been hovering in that range for awhile and we expect it to be edging up ever so slightly for the class of 2016. Yale looks at the whole package though, and we have seen plenty of candidates get in with < 700 scores.

The most important thing you should know about Yale and the GMAT?

That they don't value retesting. At least, not retesting multiple times at random without the right amount of preparation and foresight that will allow you to show real improvement. Retesting and coming up at the same score level is not going to help you. If you've taken the test twice, think carefully before doing it again if you're planning to apply to Yale.

Their admissions director Bruce DelMonico has even come out with the rather controversial statement that you should not bother retaking the GMAT if you cannot improve the total score by at least 40 points. He claims that this stance is based on the GMAC dataset of average improvement in scores when people test multiple times. Please realize that this opinion is NOT shared by most other admissions directors at top MBA programs (we've asked them). This should be taken into account for your overall strategy at Yale.

Does this mean that it's OK to submit an app with a low score, since you don't have the confidence that you'll increase it by that much?

With the ~715 average score and a relatively small class size, then we can surmise that the answer is "no." If you've only tested once and your score is <700, then we strongly suggest you try again.

Yale doesn't have such a large class that they can absorb more than a handful of students with lower GMATs. At the same time, they often attract the non-traditional candidates who tend to have lower scores. So they can be flexible. Don't get too bunched up about your score.

Or, if you want to take another approach: If your score is lower, and you're committed to Yale as your school of choice, then buck up and do the studying required to raise that test score up.

As a rule of thumb, you should aim to be above the 60th percentile for quant. There are no cut-offs and they will absolutely consider your candidacy even if you're below that – but a 60th percentile is indeed low for the math side. SOM admissions has said that scores in the 70th percentile and higher would "put you in a stronger position." SOM admits skew higher on verbal so again, they can be flexible on where your score ends up.

If you want to get your application in yet you have plans to retake the GMAT in between rounds, then communicate this to Yale on your application (there may be a place in this year's app to indicate this, and if not, then include it in the optional essay). Tell them the date that your next test is scheduled for. Make sure you follow up with them after you test; you need to do so even if your score wasn't what you had hoped. The adcom at Yale will usually try to accommodate this situation and will hold off on final judgment on your candidacy until that new score is received. Not all schools are willing to do this, so this shows you Yale's interest in helping you be successful based on this flexibility they offer.

Another place where Yale is flexible: The five-year cut-off point on age of GMAT test. The general guideline in applying to any business school is that your GMAT (or GRE) must be a recent test, within the past five years. How each school calculates that five-year window is different; some schools calculate it up to the time of matriculation (next fall), while others need it to be valid only at the time of application. The Yale admissions team has told us that they can be accommodating on this point. If your score is from a test that was awhile back, then contact admissions to see if it's going to be valid for your app this year. The main reason that they may prefer to see a more recent score is only because older ones don't have the Integrated Reasoning component (see next paragraph), but this alone isn't typically reason to force a retest. See what admissions says before proceeding – but be sure to have that same conversation with every school you're interested in, since their policies do vary significantly on this matter.

Starting with the 2014-'15 season, Yale plans to put more emphasis on the Integrated Reasoning section of the GMAT. They are one of the first schools to start paying attention to this component of the test. Yale works closely with GMAC (many other schools do too but Yale seems to have a closer connection than some) and they are doing joint studies on correlation between the IR and grades. They already know that the AWA score is correlated with success at the SOM, and it's important not to dismiss that part of the test. You can get in with a slightly lower AWA but if your AWA is 5.0 or below then the adcom may scrutinize other parts of your application, and they'll especially be taking a keen interest in hearing you answer the questions in the video recording of the application that you'll complete after submission (see page 46 where we talk about this).

Another reality: As already mentioned, there seems to be a greater emphasis on GPA at Yale, so if your GMAT is a little lower, but your college marks are very strong, then it may be fine on balance. The SOM wants to see evidence that you value school and are willing to put in the work on your studies. If you did that in college then you could be in a good position even with a slightly lower GMAT score. It all gets evaluated together.

Grades

Just like with the GMAT, and just like at every school, a better academic record puts you in a stronger position when it comes to getting into Yale SOM – but in this case, it may be an even greater advantage than you'd expect. And a lower set of college marks could be a bigger drag on your candidacy than elsewhere.

The average GPA at Yale is currently around 3.55 or higher, which is a notch higher than many schools. This has been on the upswing since Dean Snyder took over. Our interpretation of it is, they understand if someone has had little business experience, or cannot do so great in a standardized testing environment, but they need to know that you'll succeed in the classroom, and the best place to find evidence of that is in the college transcript. They'll evaluate the entirety of your transcript, looking for this evidence of your abilities: the school you went to, what you majored in, the actual courses taken, and obviously the grades themselves.

One slightly different case is the military candidate. Some U.S. veterans didn't do so great in college, or maybe they went to a very challenging place like West Point, where high marks are incredibly rare. If that's you, then don't fret too much; the SOM can be understanding of such circumstances. In this case, the GMAT may have a little more weight than it might for another non-traditional candidate, just as a measure of your abilities. Again, they look at everything together. If your GPA is in the 3.0 or lower range then that's going to be much more difficult to get a "pass" by the SOM adcom – not impossible, but not that easy. This is true regardless of your background, though it might be slightly less true if you're coming to bschool from the armed forces.

If you're an international applicant, you do not need to (and should not) try to convert your marks to the American 4.0 grading system, though the adcom says that it can be helpful to provide the grading scale or standards that your school used, if that is available to you.

One thing the GMAT and your undergrad transcript are revealing to the adcom is your proficiency with quant subjects. If there's a dearth of evidence of your quant abilities in those two places, then it would be wise to show the adcom that you're prepared. Our standard advice in such cases is to take stats or micro or accounting or calculus to help demonstrate quant proficiency if your undergrad transcript doesn't reflect it. This applies to all schools, but the Yale admissions team has called this advice out specifically before, so we wanted to mention it here so you realize its importance.

Note: While a not-for-credit Coursera or other online / MOOC course can help to show your motivation and interest, such experiences typically don't have a lot of weight in the actual evaluation process. They can be a nice-to-have, but an actual course in an accredited college or university for credit and a transcript is going to help more. There are some exceptions to this on a school-by-school basis however our conservative advice is skip the MOOCs and go for a traditional course at an accredited university. No, MBAMath isn't that, either.

Bottom line: If your GPA is on the low side, then DEFINITELY be prepared to take action before applying. The EssaySnark blahg has plenty of advice on what to do about a low GPA. If your worst grades were in quantitatively difficult classes, and you also did poorly on the quant side of the GMAT, then you need to take care of that double-whammy weakness before you apply.

Older Applicant

Another area where we see Yale be more flexible at times is with the older candidate – including with Indian nationals who are past 30. That cohort tends to be trickier than most in its ability to land a spot at a top MBA program. Certain schools are more open to thirty-somethings and Yale is among them.

Yale has a dedicated track to college students which is a corollary to the HBS 2+2 program, called Yale Silver Scholars, so that shows that they are open to younger students – in the right context. For the standard full-time MBA program, then work experience is going to be almost mandatory for admission to Yale. It's possible to get in to this school with just a year or two of career experience but it's on the more unlikely side. You will have to work harder to demonstrate your reasons and prove to them why you're ready for the MBA experience now – and how you'll make a contribution in and out of the classroom.

Reapplicants

If you tried to get into bschool last year and didn't make it, then we encourage you to include Yale on your list again. They are exceedingly open to reapplicants – provided you've done something to show how you're ready now. This means that you have to put in the work to fix the glitches, and you should DEFINITELY apply in Round 1. No ifs, ands or buts, if you're a reapplicant, then do it in the first round.

If you're a reapplicant who's reading this past the Round 1 deadline, you'll still have a chance – but you've lost an advantage. Think about it from the school's perspective: You didn't make it in the first year and now you're claiming that you're wholly motivated and locked in to Yale School of Management as your #1 choice... but you couldn't get your act together to submit at the earliest deadline. It's not like you didn't have time or were working on getting a better GMAT score or something (even if you were tackling that project, there's no reason why it should've delayed your app till later in the season). The school won't hold it against you and deny if you reapply in Round 2 – it's not like you need to write an optional essay about it or something – but you're sending a stronger message if you submit at the earliest opportunity.

The SOM is as welcoming to reapplicants as any. They will want you to show how you've improved your profile, but they'll give you a fair shake and will be very open-minded when they evaluate your app this time around. The reason? Because you're showing commitment. It's nice to see someone be so dedicated. They will respond to that – provided you execute better this time.

The other reason that Yale likes reapplicants is because *they're humble.* Not getting into bschool is one of the most demoralizing things that can happen. If you were at all cocky in your assumptions about getting in the first time, then now you won't be. You'll be hungry. You'll want it more. And you're probably going to do a better job now, due to an enhanced appreciation and respect for the challenges. All of that can be appealing to the adcom; and yes, it comes through on the page.

The Yale admissions committee will review all components of your previous application along with the new materials you submit, so you'll need to go into your reapp strategy accordingly. If there are significant changes between the career goals you pitch this year compared to what you said last year, then those probably need to be explained (just as one example).

A full discussion of reapplicant strategies is beyond scope of this *SnarkStrategies Guide* however all the advice in our *Reapplicant's Guide* will serve you quite well in mapping out your second go at a Yale MBA. If you're in this boat, we wish you luck – and we have high hopes that it will turn out well.

The SOM Application

While EssaySnark is not a big fan of this trend of schools going down to a single-essay application – not because it cuts into our business (we actually saw more panicking among BSers last year when HBS first went to the single-essay app) but because one essay is just not enough to share much of who you are – we actually think that you're going to be set up just fine with Yale's.

By contrast, Wharton is making it especially tough on people this year. At least Harvard allows you to go on as long as you want with their one essay. Wharton applicants are not going to have an easy time of it. UCLA has just one essay but the question is very focused, and they give you a decent amount of space to answer it, so they're an exception, too. But generally, we feel that the single-essay app is not in anyone's best interest. It adds to the stress of applying and it can be massively frustrating to try to get all of your important stuff out into the one short document.

So when Yale announced that their app would have just one essay this year too, at first we were concerned.

And then we saw the question. And we saw that it is clear, and easy to understand, and written in a way that lets you actually dive into something important from your background. And they've given you enough space to tell a full story about it.

Which is unlike last year, when Yale had two essays, but they were confusingly-worded, so that it was hard to tell what they were looking for with each one. And both were super short.

Instead, this year's Yale application is giving you a shot at expressing yourself. It's a case where one essay is better than two.

The main reason why they can afford to go down to just one essay is, of course, the video questions that they ask with the app. (We are assuming that they're keeping those this year, too, even though they haven't breathed a word about it one way or another on their site. We wanted to get this application guide into your hands as early as possible though, so we're publishing this in June even though the Yale app itself isn't available yet.)

It's also because they ask a lot of questions in the application itself. One section of the online application covers your post-MBA interests. Believe it or not, that should be the first place you start in figuring out how to answer the main essay question.

Snarky Strategy #4

As your first task in tackling the Yale essay, go through the application and examine the entirety of the questions that they ask about.

If you're reading this essay guide right after we published it – that is, before the Yale app ha been released – then obviously you can't do this. We'll share with you below the important parts from the 2013 version of Yale's application, so you're not operating in the dark.

However, if you're reading this when most people are reading it – with deadlines fast approaching – then it will help you a lot to know what to write about in your essay if you first understand the entirety of what else the school will know about you.

Your essays should always be additive to the rest of the application. All the schools tell you that they do a holistic review of your app. Well, to help them do that the best, you need to take a holistic view of your approach.

The main reason we advocate this thorough pre-review of the application dataset is because Yale is asking about career goals in the app – just not as an essay. And everything that you present in your Yale essay should reinforce and support the rest of the application. So the goals matter, and they should be considered upfront.

Career Goals and Yale

It may not seem like it, since there's no formal essay about them, but career goals must form the foundation of your pitch to Yale SOM. It's pretty much all that they asked about in last year's essays (well, that and "why Yale"). Don't be lulled into a false sense of complacency in thinking that goals aren't important just because Yale isn't asking you to write 500 words about them this year.

Even though there's no essay on the subject, we strongly recommend that you go through and map out your goals. You'll need this to be clear in your application answers, and for your interview – and yes, for other schools. You will need to have good answers to these questions to fill out the SOM application.

As mentioned before, we're writing this guide without having seen the 2014 application, so we're going off of what was in the app for 2013 – at which time there was a question that proved confusing to some.

The SOM asked applicants:

> *What are your intended post-MBA short-term and long-term career interests?* (2 small fields provided, one for short-term, one for long-term goals)

Pretty straightforward – but then they asked:

> Please provide any additional information you feel will help us understand these career interests more fully. (150 words maximum)

An answer of 150 words is not by any stretch of the imagination an essay, yet many people took it as such. They got all twisted up about it and over-interpreted things.

From the way it's worded, we can see how some might think that follow-up question it was mandatory. But it wasn't; you could have submitted the application without including anything in that field. We know from conversations with the SOM adcom that this was only meant to allow people to explain themselves. Most people felt obligated to fill in that field – yes, even though at the time there were two other full-on essays asking about "why MBA" and "why Yale."

Let's set the record straight on this one:

Snarky Strategy #5

If your career goals are expressed appropriately, then you won't need to provide "additional information" to explain them.

Short and sweet can truly take the day – no matter what context you're asked in (formal essay, short-answer response, interview). By going through the process of defining what you want to do and why, you'll be able to construct a much more compelling presentation to the adcom, that will resonate and be supported by your Yale essay on contribution.

Many of our other *SnarkStrategies Guides* contain an exercise for helping you to define the goals before writing a traditional career goals essay. If you're applying to Columbia or Tuck or Ross or many others, you may want to pick up the strategy guides for those schools for additional insights on what needs to be present in a feasible set of goals. Even better, you can check out our Career Goals App Accelerator, with a step-by-step process of defining what needs to go into a solid set of goals for any top school, and two opportunities for feedback from EssaySnark on what you come up with.

Your Yale Essay

Finally, yes, we're going to offer suggestions for tackling this important deliverable to the SOM. Here's the question:

> *The Yale School of Management educates individuals who will have deep and lasting impact on the organizations they lead. Describe how you have positively influenced an organization—as an employee, a member, or an outside constituent.* (500 words maximum)

While we were not privy to the behind-closed-doors conversations that the Yale admissions people had during their application planning session for this year, we do know that a major filter that they use in all app evaluations is this:

Have you done something significant in your life?

That's what they want to learn about you. We've even heard that that's the favorite component for admissions officers to discover.

The "significant" angle is up to you to define. It's not technically a part of the essay question being asked. But it will be a very useful yardstick for you to use as you sort through possible topics to present to Yale in this essay. A good Yale essay is not just about what you did that's important – though that is. It also comes down to *why* it's important, and this is an element that's self-defined. It will be up to you to express the significance of this contribution, through how you present the details of the story. When done well, it will be self-evident to the reader why you've chosen to tell them about this experience.

Two common mistakes, and tactics for dealing with them

Before we get into the details of how to approach and structure your topic for the Yale essay, we want to mention some important cautions, with a few tactics that you can consider employing after you've gotten that puppy drafted.

If you haven't written (or read) admissions essays before, then this first caution may seem downright ridiculous, but it's actually an error that many many people commit:

A Snarky Caveat

Make sure you're answering the question being asked.

You'd be surprised how often we see #essayfails based on the content in the draft not being sufficiently directed towards the question. This happens sometimes because people re-use essays for different schools' questions that aren't actually similar to each other. Other times, it just happens totally innocently: You come up with what you think is a good topic to write about, and you write about it – without going back to make sure that it actually is a fit to the question that the adcom has posed.

The other important bit of advice to toss out here at the beginning:

Be authentic.

How do you deal with these issues and avoid making such common mistakes?

It's pretty easy to do a self-assessment on your essay on the first caution, about making sure that you answer the question. You do that like this:

After you finish writing your draft, go back over it and underline the sentence(s) that directly address the essay prompt. (Sometimes it helps to set the essay aside for a day or two and then come back to it to do this test.)

If you can't easily identify the place(s) in the essay where the question is answered, it's likely that the entire essay is off track.

Errors made in the second arena, about authenticity, are harder to self-diagnose. After all, you're the one who wrote the thing, and we assume you wrote it in all earnestness. It's not like anyone ever sets out to write an *in*-authentic essay. Once it's written, how could you ever feel that it wasn't authentic? It's a tricky thing to see in one's own work.

This is where the tip offered previously (page 20) about having a friend or relative read the essay can work – though again, we caution you not to overly rely on untrained eyes for too much advice on the *content* of what you're presenting. Remember that pitching the adcoms is unlike other types of writing that people are exposed to, and even the best-intentioned advice from others can easily lead you astray.

It can be valuable to a point though, and having a friend read your draft can also help you avoid that first mistake, too. Here's how:

Give them a copy of the essay *without giving them the essay question.*

(Note: If you submit your drafts for review by EssaySnark, you should include the question at the top. Most adcoms want this too though it's less important for a school that has just one essay. But for EssaySnark's purposes, it's very helpful – not just in our reviewing of your essay, to make sure it was actually written for the correct essay question, but also when you're writing the draft – you can keep referring back to the prompt as you write, over and over again, to make sure that you're actually answering the question that they have asked.)

If you give the question-less essay to your buddy and ask them to read it, then the test is, can they figure out what the gist of the question was, just based on what you wrote in response to it? That's an excellent way to make sure that what you've written is topical.

Now, some additional Really Big Warnings are warranted here. When you're enlisting the help of a friend, they are supposed to help you by *reading it only.* They shouldn't even have a red pen in their hand when they do it. In fact, you may want to make sure they don't even *own* a red pen when they sit down to read your essay. Banish red pens from their possession. Red pens are evil. They are dangerous. They can do damage in this context.

Most people who are worth asking their opinion about a piece of writing will have a lot of trouble reading it without making corrections. But correcting it is out of scope for the assignment that you're giving them. Make yourself clear on this before handing it over.

The essay you deliver to the Yale adcom must be your own work in your own words. It's fine to get high level feedback from family or friends on how effective you are in answering the question. If they can guess what the essay question was from reading the essay itself, then you're on the right path. But they should not be writing for you. Have them look at essays without pen in hand. They should not be copyediting what you've written.

We offer these suggestions about how to make sure you've answered the question because Yale and other schools often report that they get essays submitted that are completely off. From the SOM adcom themselves: "Make sure you answer the question. We often get well written essays that are not responsive to the question that we asked."

Next: How do you write an authentic essay?

By offering an honest answer to the question. By not posturing. By not trying to second-guess the adcom.

It's easier to write about things you really care about – it sounds so much better. Don't force your answers into some pre-conceived notions of what you think the adcoms want to hear. Just be yourself.

Yale Admissions Director Bruce DelMonico put it very simply:

"If everyone writes what they think we want to hear, everybody ends up sounding the same."

As you go through the thought exercises in this *Guide* and start to develop some content for your essays, please keep this teaching in mind. Don't make stuff up in your essays. When we lay out a brainstorming exercise or tell you to work through some questions and find the answers, don't skip through it at a high level and pretend that you're done. Dive in and spend time with yourself on the material.

That's how the best content is uncovered; through a process of self-reflection and analysis. That's how you communicate who you really are to the adcom – at Yale or anywhere.

OK, let's get to it. What are you supposed to say to Yale in this essay?

The best way to go about it?

You will tell the adcom a story, which encapsulates the high moment of your career (in the recent past), that shows you being a superstar in some context – that, ideally but optionally, showcases some skills or qualities that are specifically relevant to your intended future goals.

What is the best topic to use for this essay?

While there is no trace of "career goals" lurking anywhere in the Yale essay question, it is by definition understood from how they're asking it. You did notice that first sentence, right? The one that most people may overlook as throwaway?

> **The Yale School of Management educates individuals who will have deep and lasting impact on the organizations they lead.**

What's implicit in there is the entire backstory of *the fact that you are interested in Yale* which indicates that you want to *become a leader who will have a deep and lasting impact* on some future organization. Which means, your career goals are the reason that you're applying – and they will be the main factor that Yale will use to evaluate whether to let you in. And how do you show that you're prepared to pursue those goals? By answering the essay question with an example of how you've done something impressive in the past.

Yale wants to know why you're capable and qualified to pursue this great thing you're laying out for yourself as a future path, based on who you are today, and even maybe why now is the right time. (Our Accomplishments & Achievements App Accelerator can help you identify these soundbite statements of achievement and impact if you're stuck on thinking up candidate stories.)

That's one reason why you want to keep your focus on a story that happened fairly recently. If you talk about how you had this amazing impact in an organization five years ago, well, then you're sort of saying that you were ready to go get your MBA way back then. But instead you've been hanging out for five more years. That gap would need to be bridged.

There are no hard-and-fast rules on the timeframe from which you should pull your story for this essay, however we do think a three-year window is a good one. The problem with presenting a story that is very recent is that it's unlikely that it would be "ripe" enough to use. Most projects or initiatives or corporate endeavors that show true change or "positive influence" to use the SOM's lingo are ones that require some time to put into motion. If you did something Herculean recently, then *maybe* it qualifies to be covered here – but only if you can also talk about the results.

The key word in the entire question is "influence."

How have you influenced the direction of another group of people?

How have you changed their destiny?

Oh my. When we put it that way, you freeze up. That sounds WAY too big-and-important for Little Ol' You.

But it's not, Brave Supplicant. It's not.

If you are ready for a high-powered MBA at a school like Yale, then it's a guaranteed statement that you have done something significant in this context.

Where have you:

- Brought a good idea to the table?
- Stopped a bad idea from moving forward?
- Spoken up in favor of the client's interest when the client wasn't at the table?
- Advocated on behalf of a colleague?
- Righted a wrong?
- Solved a problem?
- Brought people together?
- Innovated?

This is just the quickest of quick list that we came up with – there are a gazillion other ways to demonstrate this. "Influence" is a very soft word; you can do lots of things with it. As long as YOU feel that the thing you did is important – or wait, scratch that, a better litmus test is: *As long as OTHERS in the organization felt that what you did is important* then you have a potentially strong story to tell here.

This particular essay question lets you share yourself in action. You get to talk about literally what you have done in the workforce that's been of benefit to the organization. Where have you added value? That's what you want to explore. Did you get some kind of employee award for some project? That's going to be an obvious candidate for this essay. Did your boss gush her thanks at you for how you dealt with a customer? Again, an obvious candidate. Did you work through the weekend on yet another PowerPoint and it brought the deal home? These are all just easy examples – some of them may be a little lightweight or superficial, but any of them could possibly be candidates for sharing in this essay.

What you want to do is IDENTIFY AN EXAMPLE WHERE YOU WENT ABOVE AND BEYOND YOUR TYPICAL DUTIES.

If you talk about a project that was just like every other project that someone in your position would be assumed to do, then it's tough to see the significance. You'd need to do more to show that to the reader, to explain how or why it was important or special. The story you use in this essay should not be simply an example of how you did your normal job well. You should find something to present that shows how you went over and above what others would do.

In past years, Stanford has had some great essay questions (that they've now abandoned) that asked stuff like this:

- Tell us about a time in the last three years when you built or developed a team whose performance exceeded expectations.

- Tell us about a time in the last three years when you identified and pursued an opportunity to improve an organization.

- Tell us about a time in the last three years when you went beyond what was defined or established.

Those were a little slippery, but all of them are asking for stuff that Yale would be thrilled to hear about this year.

You do not have to show that you already have the expertise to pursue your stated future career – but you need to show how you're the kind of person who will succeed in a variety of circumstances, who will bring value to the environment, who will do what it takes to get it done. You want to demonstrate maturity and humility and resilience and ingenuity – or some other combination of positive traits and qualities that, in combination, show that you have strong potential as a leader.

Tip: The story that you present here should also be on your resume. Whatever you choose to cover in this essay is important enough that it should be easily identifiable there, too. There's plenty of other stuff that should be on the resume that may not make it into the other application assets, but this one definitely needs to be reflected in both places. By featuring it in this essay, you're communicating to the adcom that it's significant, and if it's significant, then it belongs on the resume too.

Before you start writing this essay – even before you even decide on a story you might want to use – please step back and ask yourself, *What do I want the takeaway message to be?*

What are you trying to communicate about yourself with this example from your life? Remember that we called this out with the list of attributes that Yale asks about, way back on page 1. Recognize that sometimes you need to get through a draft or two and then ask yourself this question.

You'll need to look at the messaging you're creating. What do you want the adcom to know about you as a result of this story? You should be able to review your draft and extract a specific word or two, a handful of adjectives that comprise the key ideas of the story. Add them up. Are these qualities that you think make you into a Yale MBA candidate? What do you think a complete stranger would assume to be true about the type of person you are, based on just those facts?

You may need to tweak it a little — or a lot — before you find the right story, and the right way to tell it.

How to structure it?

This essay from Yale is what's called a *behavioral question*. Many schools use these in their interviews (Stanford especially). What you need to do is tell a story in answer to this question. And the story you tell must have specifics. And you must be the star of the story. So, three criteria:

1. Tell us what happened – you need a beginning, a middle, and an end (note: this is not the same as an *intro* and a *conclusion* to the essay – you need those too!).

2. Tell us the details (without going brain-numbingly boring with them). We need context, and specifics.

3. Tell us about YOU. Other people are likely going to be involved in your story, but we need to know what you did, and the actions you took, and the results that you got.

Beyond that, this story MUST BE POSITIVE.

Even though it's asking you to talk about a time when you were dealing with negative emotions, you must identify a story to use where you transformed your frustrations into a good outcome. The hallmark of any story – whether it's from George Lucas or Garrison Keillor (you may not get that reference) or you writing an essay for the Yale adcom – is transformation. You start in one place and go to another. The lead character, and possibly many others around her, are noticeably different at the end.

There are different ways to structure the entirety of the essay, in terms of where you talk about the impact – in the beginning or at the ending – but there's really one good way to tell a story overall.

How should you write the Yale Essay?

You take a story about achievement and you communicate it the reader using a specific structure, called the STAR format. (See Wikipedia at http://en.wikipedia.org/wiki/Situation,_Task,_Action,_Result).

It's typically recommended for use in job interviews and it's perfectly appropriate for use here – as well as when you go to interview at the bschools.

The STAR format works well for essays to any school. Learn it. Use it. Love it.

EssaySnark's Guidelines for the Yale Essay

1. About two-thirds of the essay should be on storytelling, one-third on an intro and conclusion that point to why you're sharing this specific story with this specific adcom.

2. We *strongly* recommend only using stories from the past three years. Going back any further is not advisable. There are very, very few exceptions to this.

3. As the question states, this needs to be a story where you impacted an organization – and we believe the best stories are from your career, though there might be an occasional exception to this (e.g., volunteering at a charitable organization – provided it's a significant amount of volunteering and your efforts really moved the needle; or serving as captain or coach for a sports team, etc.). For almost all applicants, we really believe that professional stories from the workplace are the best.

4. Be sure to set the context clearly at the beginning. You need to show who you were (what role/position) and who else was involved, and establish a baseline for what state the organization was in or what problem you were facing and why. This is what it means when we say "show, don't tell" - you can't just claim that you contributed, you need to explain it by laying out the scene or circumstances. Don't forget to identify the organization that you were influencing! And don't assume that the reader has studied your resume. Make it clear that this was an employer, or a volunteer gig, or whatever. Make the essay self-contained and complete; the reader shouldn't be left guessing on roles or relationships or timeframes or what have you.

5. You can go a little bit overlimit on this essay but you should try to stick to under 540 words or so (as long as you upload a file instead of doing the copy/paste into the field, then the Yale system will accept it even if it's more than 500 words, and the adcoms typically don't count words, though they always can tell at a glance when you go too much over).

6. You need an intro and a conclusion; this is a real essay, write it as such.

7. The focus needs to be on you and what you did.

8. Don't forget the outcomes too, since that's literally what they are asking about. It must be crystal clear with no interpretation needed or reading between the lines what the "influence" was that you had on this organization. Quantified results are always best. The cause→effect relationship between *what you did* and these outcomes must be obvious. A common problem we often see is people overstate the results or take credit for big outcomes without establishing how they were the contributing factor that made it happen.

By now, we've said several times that this should be a recent story, but just in case you were not listening, we will now state one specific warning in black and white: We don't recommend using stories from college (unless you're applying to the Silver Scholars program). There are going to be very, very few exceptions to this guideline. One might be: You started the alumni club at your college and have been continuously involved since graduation, and you can point to a percentage gain in donations or some other metric of alumni involvement as a direct result of your efforts.

Just because you helped launch the rugby club on campus, and the team won its division last year, doesn't mean that it's a good story to use for this essay. Put those facts down on the resume and let that suffice. Find something more recent to present in the essay.

If you don't, then you're cheating yourself of an opportunity to showcase who you are TODAY. It's great that you did those cool things in college; those count for something. But this essay must be a strategic presentation of one important achievement from your "now self." You don't want to be trudging through the history books for this one. It has to be representative of who you are today.

Getting the gist of what happened down on paper is often very challenging for people not accustomed to this type of writing. It's important to remember that your adcom reader is a) in a hurry; b) reading quickly; c) tired. And, she doesn't know you. You're a complete stranger. You need to give the right amount of detail so that we understand what you're talking about, without bogging us down in the unnecessary. Don't go digging in the dirt. Keep at a high level but give us enough context so we can understand what you're talking about. It sucks when we have to dig out the resume and study it in order to understand what a BSer is saying in an essay like this.

This is an opportunity for you to present a big win at work – if you do it right, this is an essay that will help you be remembered by your reader. Don't be flamboyant with it – be honest and accurate in how you present the information – but don't neglect to feature for us what you did and how you did it, in a way that shows that you're an overachiever who's ahead of her peers.

Can you reuse your Harvard essay for Yale?

Almost definitely not. The Yale essay is asking you to respond to a specific question. That's not at all what Harvard is asking for.

Can you reuse your Yale essay for Harvard?

Maybe.

A solid HBS application will be focused on leadership, and one important component of leadership is influence. If you do a good job of answering Yale's question, then it's very possible that that story could be used in support of a Harvard application – if appropriately tailored. You wouldn't be able to use the SOM wholesale for Harvard, but the core story? Sure, it should be strong enough that it could be repurposed (if done carefully).

Can you reuse your Yale essay for anything else?

Sure. The actually story and the way you're telling it – using the STAR structure, with a focus on results at the end – that's going to be a great value-add to most any interview you have at a top bschool. The work of constructing and polishing this story is also going to give you a valuable skill set; once you have this down, you'll be in an excellent position to tackle many other types of essays. Not all of them can use the same techniques that we covered here for crafting and structuring the content, but some of them can – and many of those will then be appropriate candidates for your inventory of stories to be trotted out in all those interviews you'll be doing.

The Optional Essay

Because the one Yale question is just one essay, which is limited, and you may feel frustrated by not being able to fit everything in, you might be tempted to slip something in through the optional essay as a way to communicate more about who you are to the adcom.

This would be a mistake.

The main uses of the optional essay are to explain why you're not getting a recommendation from your current boss, or to give them additional context around your college experience to help them understand why your grades weren't so good. Yale gives you a lot of opportunity to clarify common situations through questions asked directly in the online application – such as, please explain any gaps in employment. You should go through the actual dataset first before determining if you even need to submit an optional essay at all. Remember, it's optional. It's not meant as extra space for you to blabber on about more stories and stuff that you wanted to include in the main essay but couldn't.

Do not be tempted to write the optional essay for anything other than problems or weaknesses in your application that cannot be otherwise explained.

For almost every school in the world (MIT Sloan being one exception), the optional essay should only be used if it's *needed* – not just because it's available. Don't try to color outside the lines. Stick to the main essays, do a great job with those, and only deploy the optional essay for Yale (or any school) if it's absolutely necessary to give the adcom new information that they will need to understand your candidacy.

If you do have something critical to convey, the write it out clearly, and do it briefly. Most people don't need more than 250 words or so to say what they need to say.

It's fine to cover multiple topics in the optional essay if needed – hopefully you don't have that many weaknesses to explain, but sometimes there are, well, issues. Just be brief on everything.

Also, sorry to punt on this but in terms of the reapplicant essay: You need to get the *Reapplicant Guide* for how to prepare appropriately. We'd be doing you a disservice to try and cram in a page or so on a reapp essay here. It needs to be a reapp strategy. Hopefully you've got that book already and you're ahead of the game with it.

Recommendations

We have several resources to help you with strategizing your choice of recommenders (see the Letters of Recommendation App Accelerator) and we also offer the Recommender's Instruction Sets, which is a document that you would give to your recommenders to help them in producing a good letter on your behalf. Thankfully, fewer of you will find the need for that second product this year, because Yale and a number of other top schools have collaborated to simplify the recommendations that they require.

For 2014, Yale has just two questions that recommenders must answer, which are the same that several other schools like NYU also require. This will simplify things tremendously compared to what past-year applicants had to deal with.

Yale requires two recommendations, one of which should be from your current direct supervisor. If you cannot get a rec from that person for some reason, you must explain why in the optional essay.

Yale will also entertain an additional recommendation, but just because they allow you to submit one doesn't mean that you should. If you're considering a third rec, make sure that it's additive. It does nothing for your chances to have one more person say the same things about you. The third rec must offer a new perspective or a different angle on your candidacy that you cannot convey in any other way. You can submit this online; snail mail submissions are highly discouraged. Again, this is a rare situation where a third recommendation would be appropriate. Do not get one just because you can. It's the exception, not the rule.

If you know an SOM alum, he or she can put in a word on your behalf. Alumni get an email usually in the fall with instructions on how they can submit reference reports about current applicants. Talk to your alumni contact and let them guide you on the proper process for this (or if they're unfamiliar with how to do it, ask them to contact the school's admissions department about it).

The Yale admissions team has offered the same advice about recommendations that EssaySnark does: Don't give your recommenders anything that you've written. We've heard some admissions consultants say that you should give the recommenders your essays, but why would you do that? They should be writing about totally different subjects than you're covering yourself. It adds nothing to have your recommenders say the same things that you're already saying in your app. They need to be offering new perspectives and a different dimension on your candidacy.

Plus, even more problematic is the temptation that getting your written materials would provide. Some recommenders assume that the applicant wants them to say the same things – to the point that they might copy and paste your words into their rec form. Not good. In other cases, the recommender may simply be pressed for time and decide that it is more efficient to copy in what you said. This is all bad news for you. The same thing can happen when you provide too much background material for your recommenders; they may be tempted to re-use the materials that you gave them, either due to being rushed, or because they assume that that's what you wanted them to do by providing it in the first place. The adcoms all have a very keen sixth sense that lets them sniff out when content was written by the same person; it's almost always obvious to the reader when an applicant wrote their own rec – or in this case, innocently provided material that the recommender copied in. Even if it is innocent, it's going to be a severe mark against you if this happens. The adcoms do not like it.

Instead, here's what Yale recommends you do:

First, ask your recommender: Would you be able to submit a strong recommendation for me? Sometimes people don't and the recommendation is not positive. This is an avoidable error and it can really doom an applicant's chances.

After you're comfortable that your recommender is the right choice for the task, discuss your future plans with them. Explain to them what you're hoping to get out of bschool, and highlight any strengths or weaknesses in your app that you want them to address. These points can be fit into the first recommender question.

If your recommendation needs to be translated from another language into English, then you need to enlist someone else to do that. The best way is through a professional translation company that can certify the translation. Under no circumstances would it be appropriate for you to do the translation yourself.

All of these issues are covered in greater detail in our Letters of Recommendation App Accelerator, and you also get opportunity to submit your planned recommendation strategy to EssaySnark for private review and feedback. You can find information on this service on our website:

http://essaysnark.com/mba-admissions-consulting-services/

A last point specific to Yale: Not every school is this lenient, but the SOM allows about 10 business days after the round deadline in order to receive recommendations and supplemental information like test scores. If your recommendation isn't in on time, then you don't need to panic, though you do need to make sure it's submitted very soon.

Conversely though: If you're unable to manage the simple task of coordinating a deliverable with a senior, then the Yale admissions team may start to wonder about your readiness for bschool. Getting recommendations in on time is important, and this means starting early.

The Video Essay Questions

You are likely already well aware of the video component to an SOM application. Don't let this freak you out. It's a pretty straightforward process, all things considered. One reason that Yale was able to ditch their prior requirement for a TOEFL exam is because they rolled out the video questions, which gives them direct evidence of each applicant's English abilities. There are other value-adds to the video component too but it's something that is truly to your advantage, so don't let it freak you out.

Here's what you need to know:

1. At some point after you submit your application, you'll receive an email with instructions for the in-app video essay. In Round 1, this email will probably come out after the deadline. Yale has been playing with the timing of when the videos are done; we believe this is to try and minimize the amount of public sharing about the actual questions that candidates must answer.

2. You will log on to their site and, using the webcam on your computer, respond to a set of three separate prompts. The questions are pooled from what seems to be a fairly large database, and each person has a unique set of questions, though some do seem to get repeated regularly. This may change in the 2014 application season. These questions are not based on the elements of your application; they are just pulling at random from the population of possibilities.

3. You're allowed to do a system test before you begin the videos themselves.

4. Once you begin the session, you must complete all of them together. We didn't fully test how the system operates but we believe you can back out at any time during the system test/preview part and then still come in again later to try again. Once you start the first real question then you must finish all of them. You can't log in to resume the session later.

5. In the 2013 application, for each question, the system would provide the prompt then it allowed applicants 20 seconds to prepare an answer before beginning to record your answer. You will then have 90 seconds to present your response. IMPORTANT: It is not necessary to use up all 90 seconds! If you finish your answer early, that's absolutely fine.

A technical point: In the 2013 season, Yale's video question required Flash in the browser. This means that you probably cannot do your video question on your iPhone or iPad.

The whole process of recording your actual answers should take you under ten minutes. The process of getting ready will take you much longer! You don't want to overprepare or you risk coming across as very stiff and unnatural, but there are some steps you can take to make the process less stressful for yourself.

Sample questions from past seasons

Many of the questions asked in the SOM video prompt are what you'd expect from a standard MBA interview. You can expect one question that asks about who you are or a self-description; one behavioral question, of the "tell me about a time when" type format or "what would you do if", and one thought question where you're asked to respond to a statement that presents a particular position about the world or life.

The same techniques in preparing for an interview will serve you well for this part of the Yale process. In terms of actual questions, you can easily find what other people were asked in the 2013 application season through some simple Googling, but for convenience, here's a sample set for you to review:

- What contribution have you provided for your company?
- What accomplishment are you most proud of?
- Talk about a time when you received difficult feedback.
- If you have a conflict with your classmates, how will you resolve it?
- What is your biggest concern for the Admissions Committee in evaluating your application?
- What would your colleagues and friends say are your strengths and weaknesses?
- How would your friends and colleagues describe you?
- Please describe a creative solution that you have come up with for a problem.
- Respond to the following statement: A hero can be anyone who has attributes that people admire or try to imitate. Do you agree or disagree?
- Albert Einstein said that imagination is more important than knowledge. Do you agree or disagree?
- As business becomes more global, culture becomes less important. Do you agree or disagree?

It's important to remember that the content of your answers to these questions matters much less than your thought process in how you come up with the answer. It really is irrelevant if you don't agree with Einstein's statement; your position on that "imagination versus knowledge" idea is not critical. What matters is how you express yourself: the ideas you put forth in support of your position.

Having said that: We do not recommend overdoing it on pre-defining a set of answers to these or other questions. If you do, you run the risk of making a video that looks entirely scripted – which is missing the point of the exercise.

Here's the SOM's verbatim suggestion on how to prepare for the video questions:

> "Think about past experiences that you could talk about to use in answer for hypothetical questions. You will be prepared if you have gone through job interviews before and know your resume backwards and forwards."

General tips for the Yale SOM video essays

The hardest part of the Yale video questions is that you'll be talking to a computer – not even to another person on a webcam or through Skype, but just to a computer. That feels unnatural for many people, and it can be difficult to then *look* natural.

But don't worry about that part. The adcom knows that you may be nervous and uncomfortable.

The purpose of this exercise is that the adcom wants to get a better sense of who you are as a person, unfiltered. One reason behind schools' usage of tactics like this in the application process is to help them get a sense of who you really are. Because of the overreliance on admissions consultants by some applicants, to some extent the schools feel that they have lost touch with the actual people applying for admission. Some consultants write essays for candidates. The video question is one attempt to get at the "real you" and you may actually be doing yourself a disservice if you memorize a bunch of answers ahead of time. You want to come across as you would in an important meeting with a new client – or maybe, on a first date, where you are getting to know the other person and trying to make a good impression. There's a fine line between being a prepared version of yourself, and overdoing it. If the stuff that you find yourself saying would make your best friend laugh at you, then back off, and loosen up.

The adcom is looking for poise, thoughtfulness, and maturity in the presentation – but when we use those words, we're not talking about your physical appearance, as much as we are about your presence of mind in the answers you provide.

They do not care what you look like in the video itself. Despite that, of course we do recommend dressing up for this experience. You should at least be wearing Wall Street business casual (not Silicon Valley business casual). It would also be appropriate to wear a suit, though for some people, that will make you feel so unnatural that it might backfire. Please, no t-shirts and jeans. You are presenting yourself to the admissions committee as an accomplished young professional. You want to look the part.

Because these schools get such a large number of applicants from outside the U.S., and because some people are on slow internet connections and thus the quality of the video may not be that great, the adcoms are very forgiving in terms of the variability of how the videos look from person to person. You want to put some thought into your environment before you do the video; don't do it in a noisy location, and pay attention to what's behind you so that your background is not full of cluttered and distracting things.

And, practice! You may want to go through a formal interview prep session with us before you do the Yale video questions. Our automated interview prep is a very close approximation to the type of experience that you'll have with Yale, except that it's audio only and not a video recording. Still, we will be able to evaluate your answers using the same criteria as Yale will: looking at the content and presentation, and not how you appear. You can find more information on the automated interview prep service by EssaySnark here:

http://essaysnark.com/salespage/interviewprep/

At a minimum, you'll want to do a standard set of interview prep questions with your friends. Check out the EssaySnark site for some resources and guidance:

http://essaysnark.com/mba-interview/

Another great way to prepare: Do a practice Q&A with a friend over Skype. This will get you familiar with talking to the computer and it will make it easier when you do the real thing with the Yale system.

We're publishing a separate Video Submissions and the MBA Application strategy guide this season if you want a more extensive treatment of video submissions, including tips for setup of your space and many tools and resource for creating a video as part of an application to a school like NYU or MIT. That guide is much more detailed than you need for preparing for the Yale video question however some people who are more nervous about this part of the SOM app may want to pick it up anyway. You can find it in the EssaySnark bookstore at once it's released:

http://essaysnark.com/bookstore/

While the Yale video questions may introduce yet another point of stress into the process, they're really not a big deal. You've gone through a similar process plenty of times — granted, those were in front of an actual person who was asking you questions, rather than talking into a computer. However it's still you in the spotlight, being asked to perform — and you managed that quite well in the past. You've landed a good job or two, and you've made it to this stage in your life where you're ready for an MBA. You should do fine with this part as well.

Interviews

Even though they now have the video questions, the interview is no less important at Yale. These are typically conducted by alumni, and they're valuable to the adcom because they provide a new, third perspective on your candidacy by someone outside of the admissions team. Yale interviews are blind, meaning that your interviewer will not have read your application. They are by invitation only, so not all applicants are interviewed. However, if you get the invite, then your chances are quite high for an admit. They only invite about a third of the applicant pool to this stage of the game, yet they typically accept over 50% and often up to 60% of those who are interviewed. So it's a very good sign to get that invitation.

Still, it's not a rubber stamp, and the recommendation that your interviewer provides to the admissions board is not necessarily how they will act on your candidacy. It's very possible to do amazingly well with the interview and have a great conversation with a real rapport, and have that person recommend you whole-heartedly – and then still not get in. The opposite is also possible, and in fact quite common. Many people feel that they bombed their interview and they still get in. This is mostly due to the fact that it's near-impossible to actually tell how the interviewer is perceiving you and your responses, because of the stress of the situation and how hard it is to read complete strangers (especially when the stranger is trying not to show their cards).

In past years, interview invitations could come at any time throughout the round. Yale is trying to improve communication to candidates but they don't typically do the mid-round decision point thing where they release candidates like some other schools do.

What to Do Next

Hopefully this is enough to get you moving towards a happy application for Yale. EssaySnark reviews drafts for the top business schools on our blahg (for free!) at http://essaysnark.com. You can find instructions for submitting yours at http://essaysnark.com/contact/

If you have questions we can help with about the SOM or any of your other applications, feel free to email us at essaysnark@gmail.com or find us on Twitter (@EssaySnark).

Look for other *SnarkStrategies Guides* (digital and paperback) at your favorite bookseller or on the EssaySnark blahg.

www.ingramcontent.com/pod-product-compliance
Lightning Source LLC
Chambersburg PA
CBHW080527110426
42742CB00017B/3261